My Little Book of
Dinosaurs

by Dougal Dixon

QED

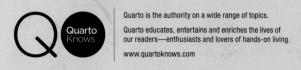

Quarto is the authority on a wide range of topics.

Quarto educates, entertains and enriches the lives of our readers—enthusiasts and lovers of hands-on living.

www.quartoknows.com

Words in **bold** are explained in the glossary on page 60.

Designed by: Punch Bowl Design
Editor: Ruth Symons
Art director: Laura Roberts-Jensen
Editorial director: Victoria Garrard

First published in the UK in 2014 by QED Publishing
Part of The Quarto Group
The Old Brewery, 6 Blundell Street, London, N7 9BH

A catalogue record for this book
is available from the British Library.

ISBN 978 1 78171 553 6

Printed in China

Contents

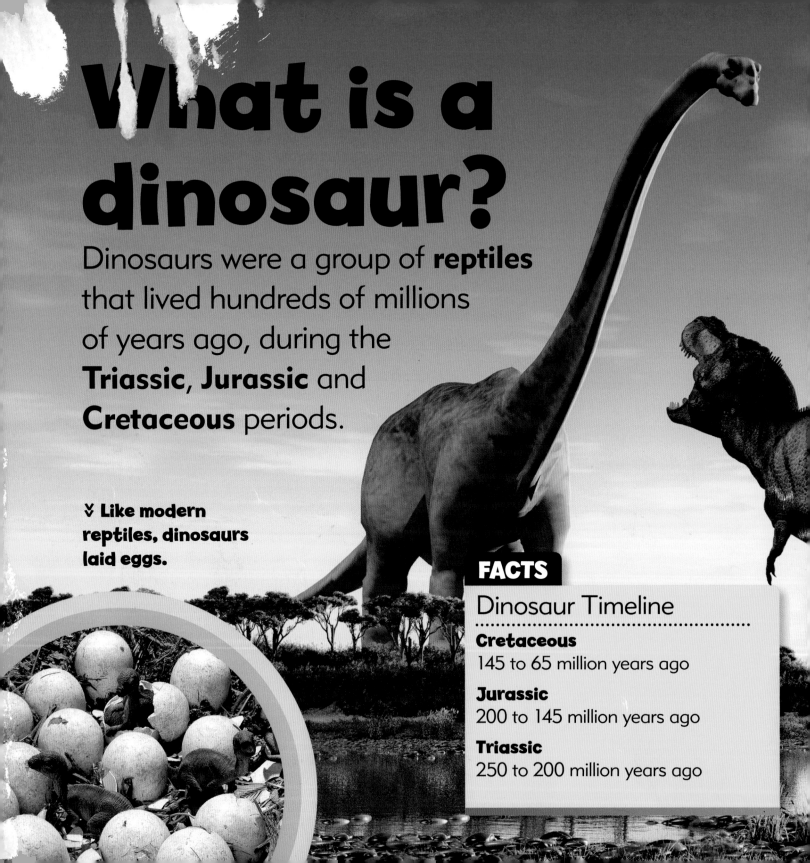

What is a dinosaur?

Dinosaurs were a group of **reptiles** that lived hundreds of millions of years ago, during the **Triassic**, **Jurassic** and **Cretaceous** periods.

⌄ **Like modern reptiles, dinosaurs laid eggs.**

FACTS

Dinosaur Timeline

Cretaceous
145 to 65 million years ago

Jurassic
200 to 145 million years ago

Triassic
250 to 200 million years ago

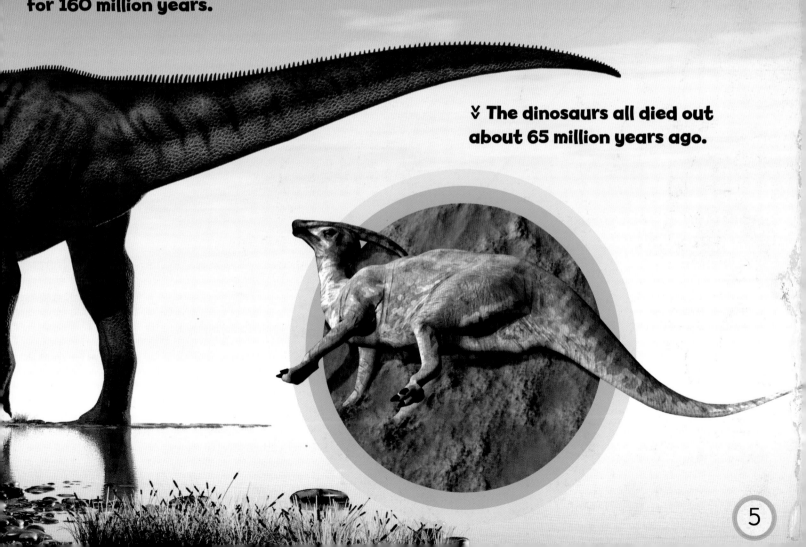

Dinosaurs came in all shapes and sizes. Some ate meat, while others ate plants. Some walked on two feet while others walked on all fours.

˅ **Dinosaurs ruled the Earth for 160 million years.**

˅ **The dinosaurs all died out about 65 million years ago.**

Coelophysis

(See-low-fy-sis)

Coelophysis was a small meat-eating dinosaur. It was only as big as a dog, but it was still very fierce.

⌄ **Astronauts took a *Coelophysis* skull into space. It was the first dinosaur in space!**

» ***Coelophysis* hunted in groups called packs.**

Coelophysis was one of the first dinosaurs. It lived in the **desert** and hunted other animals, catching them with its hands.

⌃ *Coelophysis* had sharp, jagged teeth shaped like knives.

FACTS

Coelophysis

Size
2.5 metres long

When it lived
Late Triassic, early Jurassic

What it ate
Smaller animals

Ceratosaurus

(Se-rat-oh-saw-rus)

Ceratosaurus was a huge meat-eating dinosaur with jagged horns on its head.

FACTS

Ceratosaurus

Size
6 metres long

What it ate
Other dinosaurs

When it lived
Late Jurassic

⌄ *Ceratosaurus* was big enough to hunt most big plant-eating dinosaurs of the time.

Ceratosaurus had horns on its nose and eyebrows, and a jagged crest down its back. These made it look even bigger than it really was.

>> *Ceratosaurus* had enormous, bladelike teeth.

Archaeopteryx

(Ark-ee-op-ter-ix)

Today's birds are closely related to meat-eating dinosaurs. *Archaeopteryx* was the very first bird.

>> ***Archaeopteryx*** **was about the size of a modern crow, but with a long tail.**

<< ***Archaeopteryx*** **did not have a beak. Instead it had jaws and teeth like a lizard.**

Archaeopteryx had the wings and feathers of a bird, but the head, hands and tail of a dinosaur.

⌄ *Archaeopteryx* had fingers and claws that it used for climbing trees.

FACTS

Archaeopteryx

Size
45 centimetres long

When it lived
Late Jurassic

What it ate
Smaller animals and insects

Microraptor

(Mike-row-rap-tor)

Microraptor was a tiny feathered dinosaur. It is the smallest dinosaur that has ever been found.

« *Microraptor's* back legs were covered in feathers.

FACTS

Microraptor

Size
40–60 centimetres long

When it lived
Early Cretaceous

What it ate
Insects and fish

Microraptor had feathers on its arms, legs and tail. It could not fly, but it was so small and light that it could **glide** from tree to tree.

« *Microraptors* glided through the Cretaceous forests.

13

Spinosaurus

(Spine-oh-saw-rus)

Spinosaurus was a huge meat-eating dinosaur. It mostly ate fish, which it grabbed from the riverbank.

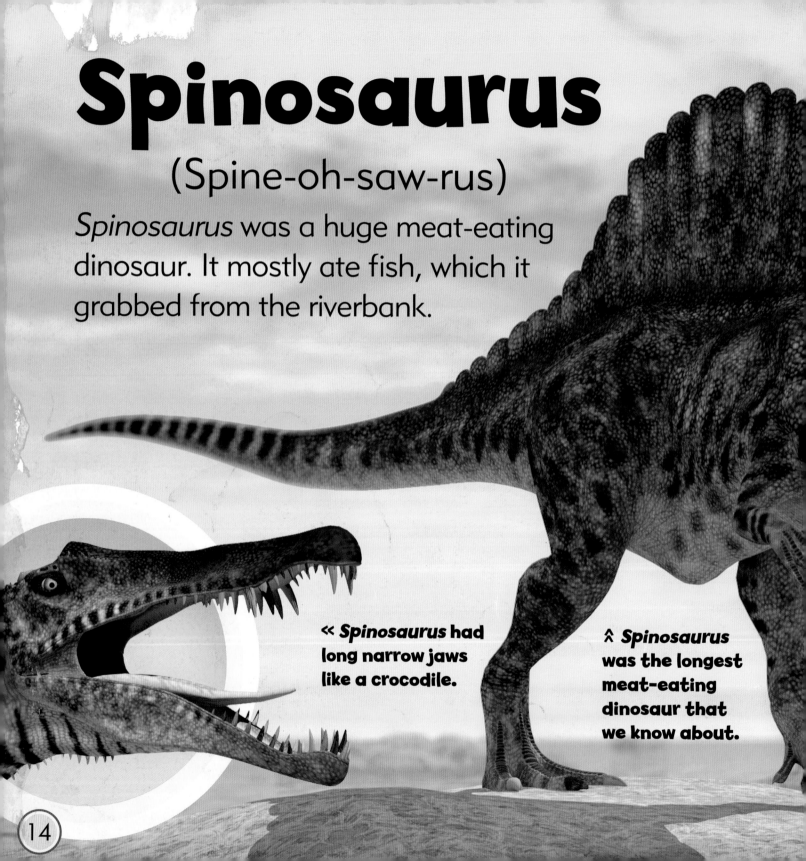

« *Spinosaurus* had long narrow jaws like a crocodile.

⌃ *Spinosaurus* was the longest meat-eating dinosaur that we know about.

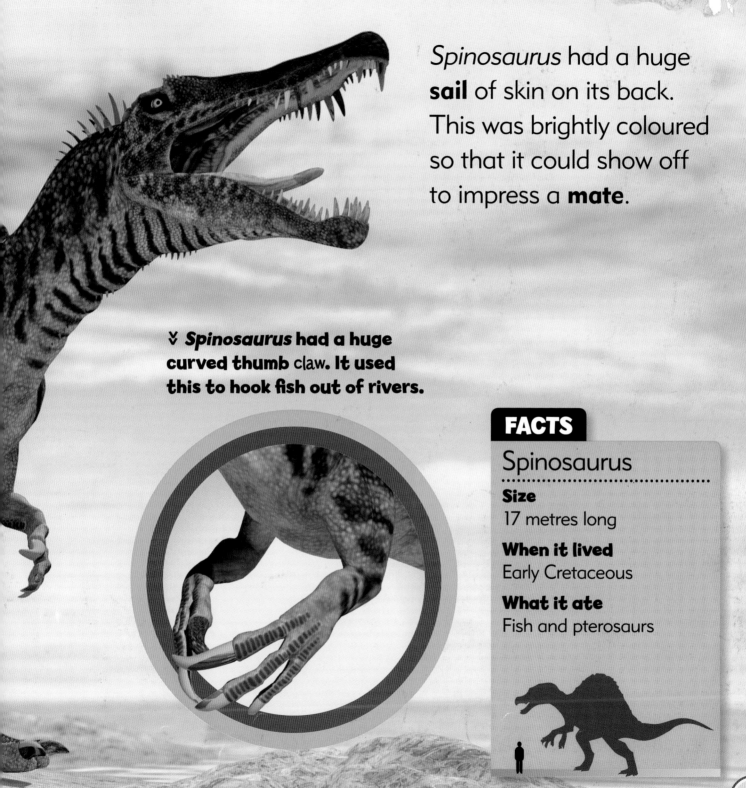

Spinosaurus had a huge **sail** of skin on its back. This was brightly coloured so that it could show off to impress a **mate**.

⌄ **Spinosaurus** had a huge curved thumb claw. It used this to hook fish out of rivers.

FACTS

Spinosaurus

Size
17 metres long

When it lived
Early Cretaceous

What it ate
Fish and pterosaurs

15

Tyrannosaurus

(Tie-ran-oh-saw-rus)

Tyrannosaurus was the biggest
meat-eating dinosaur that ever lived.

⌃ *Tyrannosaurus* **had
eyes that faced
mainly forwards. This
helped it to spot** prey.

« *Tyrannosaurus* killed its prey with its huge bladelike teeth.

Tyrannosaurus walked on two strong back legs. It prowled the forests of North America hunting, killing and eating other big dinosaurs.

FACTS

Tyrannosaurus

Size
12 metres long

When it lived
Late Cretaceous

What it ate
Other dinosaurs

» Despite its huge size, *Tyrannosaurus* had tiny arms.

Velociraptor

(Vel-oss-ee-rap-tor)

Velociraptor was the size of a fox and a deadly killer. It had a long, sharp claw on each back foot.

⌄ ***Velociraptor* hunted in packs. This meant it could hunt dinosaurs much bigger than itself.**

FACTS

Velociraptor

Size
2 metres long

When it lived
Late Cretaceous

What it ate
Other dinosaurs

In a fight, *Velociraptor* held on to its prey with its big hands and slashed it to death with the killer claws on its feet.

>> **When *Velociraptor* walked, it lifted its claws up and away from the ground.**

Oviraptor

(Oh-vee-rap-tor)

Oviraptor was a small dinosaur with feathers and a beak. It looked a bit like a bird.

⌄ *Oviraptor* made nests in the sand, and sat on its eggs to keep them warm.

FACTS

Oviraptor
....

Size
1.8 metres long

When it lived
Late Cretaceous

What it ate
Eggs and small animals

Oviraptor raided the nests of other dinosaurs. It would grab eggs in its big hands and break into them with its beak.

⌃ *Oviraptor* had a beak like a bird's, but with tiny teeth on the roof of its mouth.

Diplodosaurus

(plat-ee-oh-saw-rus)

Most of the dinosaurs were plant-eaters. The earliest plant-eaters, like *Plateosaurus*, had long necks.

FACTS

Plateosaurus

Size
8 metres long

When it lived
Late Triassic

What it ate
Plants

« *Plateosaurus* used its long neck to reach food in the treetops.

Plateos... the Triassi... It travelled a... **herds** looking fo... to eat and water to drink.

⌄ *Plateosaurus* could walk on two legs or on all fours.

23

plodocus

(Dip-lo-do-kus)

Diplodocus was a long-necked plant-eating dinosaur. It was one of the longest dinosaurs ever.

FACTS

Diplodocus

Size
27 metres long

When it lived
Late Jurassic

What it ate
Low-growing plants, or leaves from the trees

⩔ *Diplodocus* lived on wide, open plains, feeding on leaves in the trees.

Diplodocus had a long, low-slung neck. It could use its tail like a whip, to scare away **predators**.

>> *Diplodocus* could probably stand on its back legs to reach the tops of trees.

Brachiosaurus

(Brak-ee-oh-saw-rus)

Brachiosaurus was one of the tallest long-necked plant-eaters. It held its head in an upright position, a bit like a giraffe.

>> **Brachiosaurus had a long neck that made up half of its height.**

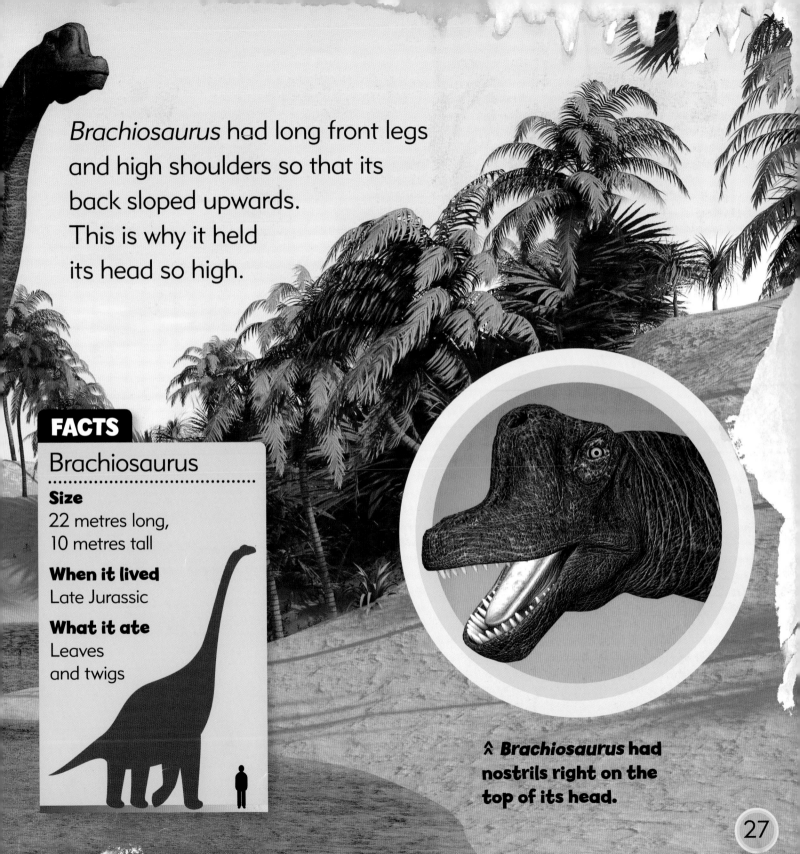

Brachiosaurus had long front legs and high shoulders so that its back sloped upwards. This is why it held its head so high.

FACTS

Brachiosaurus

Size
22 metres long,
10 metres tall

When it lived
Late Jurassic

What it ate
Leaves
and twigs

⌃ *Brachiosaurus* had nostrils right on the top of its head.

27

argasaurus

(A*m*-are-gar-saw-rus)

Amargasaurus was one of the long-necked plant-eating dinosaurs. It lived in South America.

« *Amargasaurus* had teeth like a comb. They were used for raking leaves from branches.

˅ **Two rows of spines made *Amargasaurus* look scary.**

Amarga... ...d a double ...w spines down it ...neck, and a low sail along its back. The spines and sail were used to attract a mate.

« **If an adult human stood beside *Amargasaurus*, they would come up to its hip.**

FACTS

Amargasaurus
....

Size
10 metres long

When it lived
Early Cretaceous

What it ate
Plants

Argentinosaurus

(Ah-gen-teen-oh-saw-rus)

Argentinosaurus was the biggest and heaviest dinosaur ever discovered.

⌃ *Giganotosaurus* **was one of the only meat-eaters big enough to threaten** *Argentinosaurus*.

Argentinosaurus spent most of its life eating. It had to take in a lot of food to keep its huge body healthy.

⌃ **Argentinosaurus was as big as a blue whale!**

FACTS

Argentinosaurus

Size
30 metres long

What it ate
Plants

When it lived
Late Cretaceous

Iguanodon

(Ig-wan-oh-don)

Iguanodon was a large plant-eating dinosaur. It usually walked on four legs but could stand or run on two.

FACTS

Iguanodon

Size
10 metres long

When it lived
Early Cretaceous

What it ate
Plants

∧ *Iguanodon* had a narrow beak for snipping off leaves.

✻ *Iguanodon* **lived in herds around** swamps.

Iguanodon could eat low-growing plants or it could sit back on its hind legs to reach leaves in the trees.

✻ *Iguanodon* had a sharp thumb spike for ripping down leaves or fighting off enemies.

Ouranosaurus

(Oo-ran-oh-saw-rus)

Ouranosaurus was a big two-footed plant-eater with a large sail on its back.

⌄ *Ouranosaurus* used its brightly coloured sail to help attract a mate.

FACTS

Ouranosaurus

Size
7 metres long

When it lived
Early Cretaceous

What it ate
Leaves and twigs

The sail was made up of long bony spines sticking out of the backbone, and covered in skin. It probably helped *Ouranosaurus* to warm up in the sun.

⋀ *Ouranosaurus* had a broad beak, like a duck's.

Parasaurolophus
(Par-ah-saw-roll-off-us)

Parasaurolophus was a plant-eating dinosaur with a hollow **crest** that swept back from its head.

⌄ *Corythosaurus*, a relative of *Parasaurolophus*, had a crest shaped like a helmet.

« *Parasaurolophus* used its crest as a trumpet to make a loud noise!

» *Olorotitan* had a crest shaped like an axe blade.

Several dinosaur **species** had crests on their heads. They were all different shapes and colours so that dinosaurs could tell each other apart.

FACTS

Parasaurolophus

Size
10 metres long

When it lived
Late Cretaceous

What it ate
Plants

Stegosaurus

(Steg-oh-saw-rus)

Many plant-eating dinosaurs were covered in **armour**, or had plates or **horns** to protect themselves.

FACTS

Stegosaurus

Size
9 metres long

What it ate
Plants

When it lived
Late Jurassic

˅ *Stegosaurus* had four long spikes on its tail. It could use these to fight off meat-eating dinosaurs.

Stegosaurus had a double row of plates down its back. These guarded it from attacks. They were also used for showing off to impress other dinosaurs.

≫ *Kentrosaurus* was a smaller relative of *Stegosaurus.*

Ankylosaurus

(An-kie-low-saw-rus)

Ankylosaurus was a large, plant-eating dinosaur, covered in bony armour.

>> *Ankylosaurus was the biggest of all the armoured dinosaurs.*

40

⌃ *Ankylosaurus* had a huge bony club on the end of its tail.

⌃ *Ankylosaurus* even had armoured eyelids.

It had armour plates on its head, neck and tail. These were made of bone covered in horn and protected *Ankylosaurus* from predators.

FACTS

Ankylosaurus

Size
11 metres long

When it lived
Late Cretaceous

What it ate
Plants

Triceratops

(Try-sair-a-tops)

Triceratops was a four-footed plant-eater with a neck shield and horns on its face.

FACTS

Triceratops

Size
9 metres long

When it lived
Late Cretaceous

What it ate
Plants

⌃ *Triceratops* had a big beak used for snipping off bits of food.

Triceratops was a bit like a modern rhinoceros. It had a big body, thick legs and horns on its face. Like a rhinoceros, it ate low-growing plants and leaves from bushes.

>> **Styracosaurus was a horned dinosaur with long spikes around its neck shield.**

Stegoceras

(Steg-oh-sair-ass)

Stegoceras was a small, plant-eating dinosaur with an armoured dome on its head.

« *Stegoceras* looked brainy because of its big head. But its dome was made of solid bone!

Stegoceras lived in herds. Males sometimes fought each other to see who would lead the herd. They would headbutt each other on the legs to see who was stronger.

⌃ *Stegoceras* used its head to fight off rivals or enemies.

FACTS

Stegoceras

Size
3 metres long

When it lived
Late Cretaceous

What it ate
Plants

Rhamphorhynchus

(Ram-for-ink-us)

At the time of the dinosaurs, the skies were full of flying reptiles called **pterosaurs**.

⌃ *Rhamphorhynchus* **had a long tail, with a flap on the end, which it used for steering.**

Rhamphorhynchus was one of the earliest pterosaurs. It had a hairy body and long, leathery wings. Each wing was supported by one enormous finger.

⌃ *Rhamphorhynchus* had sharp teeth for snatching up fish as it flew low over water.

⌃ *Rhamphorhynchus* had a body the size of a crow, but with long narrow wings.

FACTS

Rhamphorhynchus

Size
1.75-metre wingspan

When it lived
Late Jurassic

What it ate
Fish and squid

Quetzalcoatlus

(Ket-zal-coe-at-lus)

As time went by, the pterosaurs became bigger and bigger. *Quetzalcoatlus* was as big as an aeroplane!

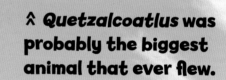

ʌ *Quetzalcoatlus* was probably the biggest animal that ever flew.

« When it was on the ground, *Quetzalcoatlus* walked on all fours and was as tall as a giraffe.

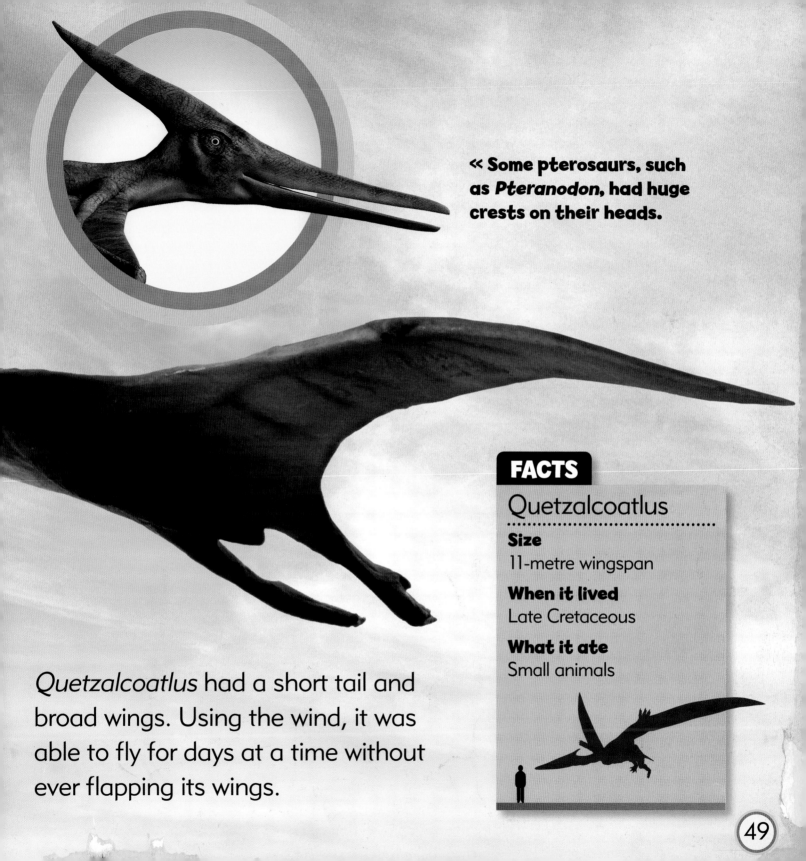

« **Some pterosaurs, such as *Pteranodon*, had huge crests on their heads.**

FACTS

Quetzalcoatlus

Size
11-metre wingspan

When it lived
Late Cretaceous

What it ate
Small animals

Quetzalcoatlus had a short tail and broad wings. Using the wind, it was able to fly for days at a time without ever flapping its wings.

Plesiosaurus

(Ple-si-oh-saw-rus)

While dinosaurs roamed the land, the seas were full of swimming reptiles.

« *Liopleurodon* had a big head and short neck, like a modern whale.

˅ **Plesiosaurus** had long, sharp teeth – ideal for catching slippery fish.

FACTS

Plesiosaurus

Size
3.5 metres long

What it ate
Fish

When it lived
Early Jurassic

Plesiosaurus swam through the seas and oceans, using its big **flippers**. It had a long neck that could reach out to snap up fish.

Ichthyosaurus

(Ick-thee-oh-saw-rus)

Ichthyosaurus was a small, fishlike reptile with a long, pointed **snout**.

« *Ichthyosaurus* ate fish and ammonites – animals that lived in spiral shells.

Ichthyosaurus looked and lived just like a fish. It had a streamlined shape and pointed fins on its back and tail.

⌄ **The name *Ichthyosaurus* means 'fish lizard'.**

FACTS

Ichthyosaurus
....

Size
2 metres long

When it lived
Early Jurassic

What it ate
Fish and ammonites

⌃ *Ichthyosaurus* **had huge eyes for hunting in deep, dark waters.**

Mosasaurus

(Mow-za-saw-rus)

Mosasaurus was one of the biggest reptiles swimming in the oceans. It preyed on seabirds, large fish and other sea reptiles.

« *Mosasaurus* was the terror of the seas at the end of the Cretaceous period.

« *Mosasaurus* had such strong jaws that it could crush turtle shells.

Mosasaurus had a body shaped like a crocodile's, but with powerful flippers instead of arms and legs. It had a long snout lined with sharp teeth.

FACTS

Mosasaurus

Size
18 metres long

When it lived
Late Cretaceous

What it ate
Fish, ammonites and other swimming reptiles, such as turtles

How fossils form

We know all about dinosaurs thanks to **fossils** – pieces of dinosaur bone preserved in rocks.

1

2

3

>> **There are also fossils of dinosaur footprints, eggs and even droppings.**

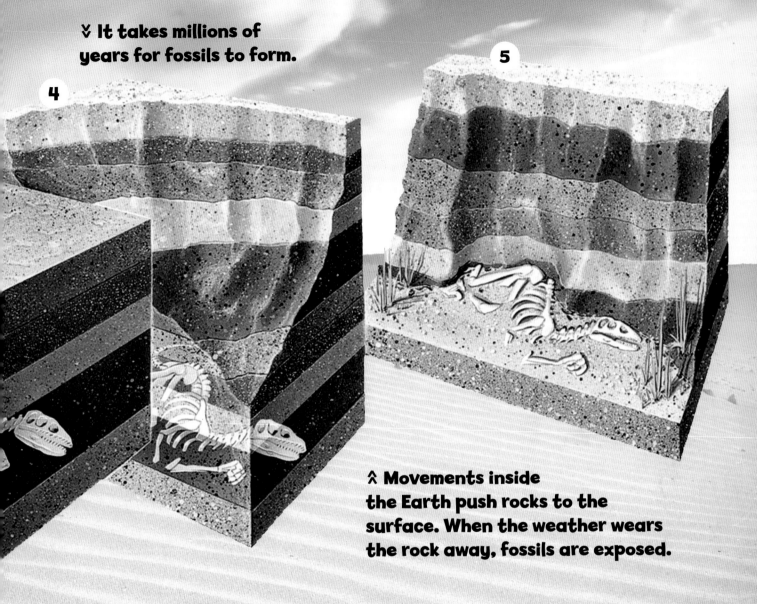

⌄ **It takes millions of years for fossils to form.**

4

5

⌃ **Movements inside the Earth push rocks to the surface. When the weather wears the rock away, fossils are exposed.**

Fossils formed when a dinosaur's remains were covered quickly by mud or sand. As the mud and sand was packed down over time, it turned into rock. Inside the rock, the dinosaur's bones turned to stone.

Dinosaurs today

It takes a lot of work to get a fossil out of the ground and into a museum!

⌄ **Scientists that study dinosaurs are called** palaeontologists.

∧ **This is a dinosaur skeleton mounted in a museum.**

Most museums make models of fossils to use in their displays. The original fossils are kept safely behind the scenes for scientists to study.

⋎ Scientists study fossils closely to learn how dinosaurs lived.

5

Glossary

armour A protective covering.

claw A curved, pointed toenail on an animal. Some dinosaurs used their sharp claws as a weapon.

crest A bony growth on an animal's head or back.

Cretaceous The period of time between 145 and 65 million years ago. The dinosaurs died out suddenly at the end of the Cretaceous.

desert A dry place that gets very little rain.

flipper A flat, paddle-shaped limb used for swimming.

fossil The remains of something that lived a long time ago, now turned to stone in the rock.

glide To fly without flapping.

herd A large group of animals that live together.

horn A hard, pointed growth on an animal's head.

Jurassic The period of time between 200 and 145 million years ago.

mate An animal's partner for breeding.

pack A group of animals that live and hunt together.

palaeontologist A scientist who studies ancient animals and plants.

predator An animal that hunts other animals for food.

prey An animal that is hunted by a predator.

pterosaur A flying reptile that lived at the time of the dinosaurs.

reptile A cold-blooded animal that usually lives on land and lays eggs.

sail A sail on a dinosaur's back was like a fin on a fish's back.

snout The nose and jaws of an animal.

species A group of animals that look like each other and can breed together.

swamp An area of land that is always wet and flooded.

Triassic The period of time between 250 and 200 million years ago. The first dinosaurs appeared at the end of the Triassic.

Index

Picture credits

Alamy
3 leonello calvetti, 11r Daniel Eskridge / Stocktrek Images, 28-29c Sergey Krasovskiy / Stocktrek Images, 34-35 Walter Myers / Stocktrek Images, 35 Craig Brown / Stocktrek Images, 41t Darby Sawchuk, 42-43c Leonello Calvetti, 43 Friedrich Saurer, 48-49 Engel & Gielen / LOOK Die Bildagentur der Fotografen GmbH, 52l Ellen McKnight, 54-55c Sergey Krasovskiy / Stocktrek Images, 58-59 Javier Etcheverry, 58b Ray Nelson / PHOTOTAKE, 59br WaterFrame

Getty
fc Roger Harris, 32-33c Andy Crawford

Mark Witton
48bl © Mark Witton 2011-2013

Science Picture Library
4b Natural History Museum, London, 5b Jose Antonio Peñas, 6bl Gary Hincks, 7tr Natural History Museum, London, 18-19 Jose Antonio Peñas, 19tr Roger Harris, 20-21c Julius T Csotonyi, 21c Julius T Csotonyi, 32l Natural History Museum, London, 33br Natural History Museum, London, 50-51 Roger Harris, 52-53 Christian Darkin, 54l Jaime Chirinos, 63 Natural History Museum, London, 64 Julius T Csotonyi

Shutterstock
bctl DM7, bctc Ozja, bctr Linda Bucklin, bcc Bob Orsillo, bcbl Esteban De Armas, bcbr Catmando, 1l Catmando, 1r Michael Rosskothen, 1b Bob Orsillo, 2 Michael Rosskothen, 4-5 iurii, 6b nrt, 6-7 Michael Rosskothen, 8-9 Videowokart, 8-9c DM7, 9br Bob Orsillo, 10bl Linda Bucklin, 10-11c Andreas Meyer, 10-11 DemianM, 12-13 Serg64, 13r Dariush M, 12b Michael Rosskothen, 13c Michael Rosskothen, 14l Kostyantyn Ivanshen,14-15 Kostyantyn Ivanyshen, 15bl Kostyantyn Ivanyshen, 16-17 Yuriy Kulik, 16l DM7, 16-17c DM7, 17br Kostyantyn Ivanyshen, 20-21 Laborant, 22-23 Videowokart, 22-23 Michael Rosskothen, 23br Linda Bucklin, 24-25 Catmando, 25br Michael Rosskothen, 26-27 Kostyantyn Ivanyshen, 27c Bob Orsillo, 28-29b Mares Lucian, 28b Michael Rosskothen, 30b Michael Rosskothen, 30-31 Elenarts, 32-33 JuneJ, 36b Linda Bucklin, 36-37 Curioso, 36-37c Jean-Michel Girard, 37tr Catmando, 38-39 ragnisphoto, 38-39c leonello calvetti, 39 Kostyantyn Ivanyshen, 39c Bob Orsillo, 40-41 yanikap, 41 Catmando, 42-43 haraldmuc, 44-45 nrt, 44bl Michael Rosskothen, 44-45c Michael Rosskothen, 46l Michael Rosskothen, 46-47 Iakov Kalinin, 46-47c Linda Bucklin, 48-49 Serg64, 49l Bob Orsillo, 50l Michael Rosskothen, 54-55 Rich Carey, 56-57 Zeljko Radojko, 56r Celiafoto, 61br DM7, 62 Bob Orsillo